st Printing, 2025.

3N: 978-1-951573-53-9

ww.educatelearners.com

I Feel

HAPPY

CALM

EXCITED

FOCUSED

What can I do?

Smile

Have Fun

Laugh

Do things
I like

Say
I'm
Happy

I Feel

SAD

SICK

ASHAMED

LONELY

What can I do?

Do a new activity

Ask for support

Think good thoughts

Do things I like

Say I'm Sad

I Feel

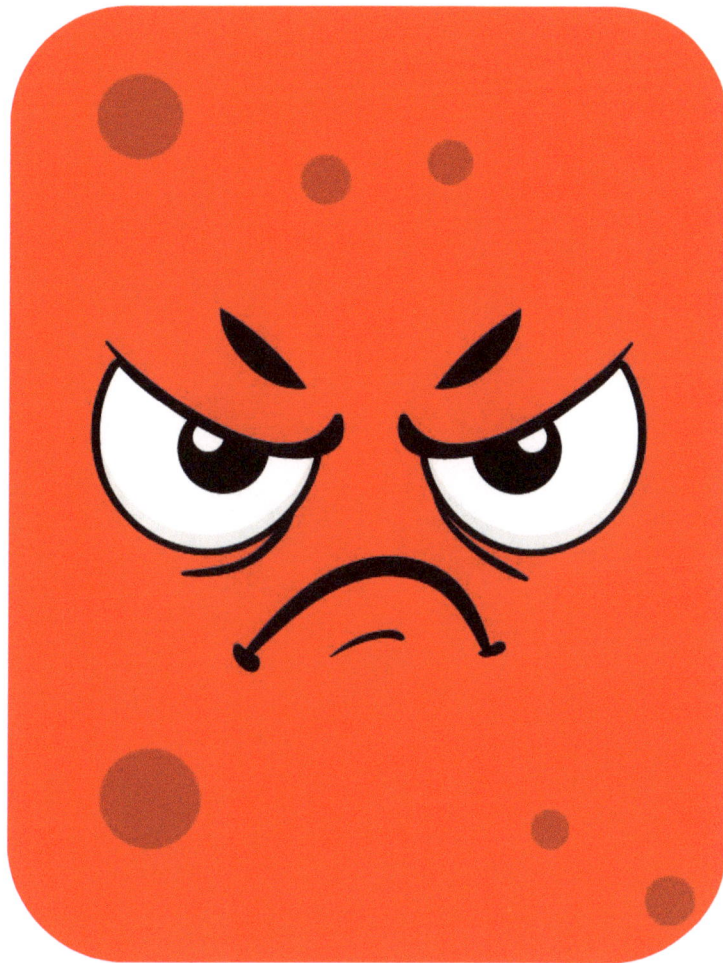

MAD

FRUSTRATED

IRRITATED

UPSET

What can I do?

Do a calming strategy

Do things I like

Ask for a break

Take a walk

Say I'm Mad

I Feel

SCARED

SHOCKED

SURPRISED

DISGUSTED

What can I do?

Do a calming strategy

Take a Walk

Ask for a break

Do things I like

Say I'm Scared

I Feel

CONFUSED

PUZZLED

DAZED

STUMPED

What can I do?

Ask A Question

Look Up info

Ask for help

Find out more info

Say I'm Confused

I Feel

WORRIED

NERVOUS

UNSURE

CONCERNED

What can I do?

Think good thoughts

Do a calming strategy

Do things I like

Do a new activity

Say I'm Nervous

I Feel

TIRED

SICK

EXHAUSTED

SLEEPY

What can I do?

Take a
break

Go sit
down

Go to
sleep

Drink
water

Say
I'm
Tired

THANK YOU FOR READING!

Get a free year long subscription to our online education resource library when you purchase any one of our books.

Code: EDBOOKS

educatelearners.com